60
BIBLICAL TRUTHS

60
BIBLICAL TRUTHS

An Essential Medicine In Times of Turmoil

Sean R Exeter

Xulon Press
2301 Lucien Way #415
Maitland, FL 32751
407.339.4217
www.xulonpress.com

Printed in the United States of America.

ISBN-13: 978-1-63221-261-0

THIS BOOK BELONGS TO:

Name:

TABLE OF CONTENTS

IN THESE UNCERTAIN TIMES, IT IS EASY TO BECOME distracted by the signs we see, an indulge ourselves in a way that seems to want to take the weight of the world on our shoulders. A burden we were never meant to carry.

In society today I believe it is fair to say, as a human being we all are in some way in pursuit of happiness no matter how each individual defines that.

Over the years, I have learnt that it is true that your words do have a tendency to promote life and death, Blessings and curses, and like a toxic cocktail of some sort your words can become that detriment not just to your state of mind, but have a reverberant effect on how you live and see life in general.

The word is clear it says in Deut 30:19(NIV) This day I call the earth as witnesses against you that I have set before you life and death, Blessings and curses now choose life, so that you and your family may live. The truth is, any reasonable person might not have to be told twice if their lives and their families lives depended on that later statement, yet it's astonishing as to how many people say they value life yet live in a pathway of self-destructive behavior. I've long contemplated the need to write this book, because at one point in my own life, I've engaged in behavior that's unbecoming who I am today, and I've reversed that by engaging in Spiritual truths, that I believed has kept my life from destruction.

I realize that being responsible, staying teachable humble and speaking the Word daily, God has kept that solid ground beneath my feet and he'll do the same for you. Ps 107:20(NIV) says he sent his word and healed them, and delivered them from their destructions. The word also says even to your old age and gray hairs, "I am he who will sustain thee. "I have made you and I will carry you." Isa 46:4.

Is that you today? Wherever we are in life, I proclaim to you God's word is like Medicine. I have also come to realize how essential Biblical truths are. When I was younger doing whatever, an even in the midst of destructive behavior, I declared Psalms 121 over my life as if as a regimen. I know it kept me and brought me home safe and sound over the years even though I felt I shouldn't have made it. I also declared his word being that lamp at my feet and a light on my path Ps 119:105. Today I encourage you to use these scriptures, Pray and apply them like medicine. Memorize one scripture a day. I believe and declare that it would have a tremendous effect on your life in more ways than one for God is no respecter of persons. Acts 10:34(NIV)

ANXIETY

Do not be anxious about anything, but in every situation, by prayer and supplication, with thanksgiving, present your requests to God. **~~ Phil 4:6 NIV**

AS I'VE STATED IN MY INTRODUCTION WE DO LIVE in uncertain times, but nothing we face today, be it a virus, the economy. Diabetes may have a name; cancer may have a name this Covid-19 pestilence may have a name. But nothing we face today, regardless of the situation is bigger, or more powerful than the name that's above every name. Our Lord and savior Jesus Christ. As we all grieve with the families of loved ones succumbed to this unprecedented tragedy, our country had ever seen with lives claimed now topping 100,000. Our hearts and prayers go out to all the families involved. But I do believe there is a shaking that's about to shift things in position the likes we've never seen. But be not anxious for nothing, by prayer requests and thanking God let him know your need.

Prayer ~~ Lord I thank you that according to Phil 4:6 I relinquish all anxiety about any situation or circumstances I face today. Regardless of what it looks like you still sit on the thrown of my life and I decree that all will be well, I have the mind of Christ and I hold the thoughts feelings and purposes of your heart in the mighty name of Jesus Amen!!

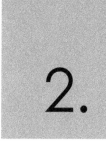

2.

WITH GOD ALL THINGS ARE POSSIBLE

Jesus looked at them and said, "With man this is impossible, but not with God; all things are possible with God." ~~ **Mark 10:27 NIV**

ONE OF THE THINGS WE OFTEN DO IS LIMIT GOD AS to what and how much he can do; that's why at times we exclude him or probably don't even acknowledge him or his input where our business is concerned. In an effort, what you're really saying is I got this Lord. Big mistake; what we ought to be saying is Lord I do recognize your mighty hand for nothing is too hard for you.

Prayer ~~ Father forgive me for the times that I thought I can handle everything on my own. Lord I recognize you are a sovereign God and there may be little details about situations I know nothing of. I free myself to be teachable to the Holy Spirit, paying attention to that still small voice in the Mighty Name of Jesus Amen!!

3.

YOU WILL HAVE WHAT YOU SAY!

Jesus replied, " Truly I tell you, if you have faith and do not doubt, not only can you do what was done to the fig tree, but also you can say to this mountain, 'Go, throw yourself into the sea, 'and it will be done. **Matt 21:21 NIV**

I BELIEVE THIS IS SIMPLY A TEST OF YOUR FAITH AND belief in God. There is so many definitions of faith, but I like to think that your faith is a practical expression of confidence that you have in God and in his word" …it's not just believing that God can it's actually knowing that he will. It's trusting him when life doesn't seem to make sense. Ever been there?

Prayer ~~ Lord I thank you that because of my faith I believe that what I say and believe will come to past. I command my words to take effect, the minute I believe in Jesus Name Amen!!

SEEK GOD'S KINGDOM FIRST

But Seek first his kingdom and his righteousness, and all these things will be given to you as well. Matt 6:33 NIV

THIS SCRIPT MOVES ME EVERY TIME. WHEN JESUS made that statement, it was really a directive aimed at our humanity, that if God can even clothe the grass of the fields which is here today and tomorrow is thrown into the fire...won't he not more clothed you, you of little faith. Let us not be so consumed of what we need to eat or drink; or about your body, what you will wear. Is not life more than food, and the body more than clothes? Allow me a millennial moment. Yes, your Father's got this. It's really important that we understand that our God knows what we're in need of. He's not a blind or absent-minded dad but we need to seek him first. Yes, he wants to be involved in all that you do. Let him take residence in the driver's seat of your life, that navigational system that does not promote errors.

Prayer ~~ Lord I thank you that I can rely on you to be my navigational systemic direction at all times. Lord I also realize that my life, my times are in your hands because you called my end from the beginning, I am in agreement that I will seek and be guided by your word at all times in Jesus name Amen!!

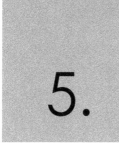

5.

APPLY GOD'S WISDOM

God can fill you with the knowledge of his will in all wisdom and Spiritual understanding... see **Col 1:9 NIV**

WHEN FALSE TEACHINGS INFILTRATED THE CHURCH at Collosse apparently adding and subtracting elements that would be a detriment to their well-being. The apostle Paul wrote this letter reminding Christians of the superiority of Jesus over religious regulations, even Jewish rules at the time, in an effort to curb their beliefs. Keeping their minds stayed on Jesus. In Colossians 1:9 he reminds them that he will continue to ask God to fill them with the knowledge of his will in all wisdom and Spiritual understanding, that the Spirit gives. We ourselves need a constant reminder of who we serve and who's we are. The devil is out there like a roaring lion seeking on who to consume 1 Pet 5:8 . Be vigilant.

Prayer~~ Lord I don't always know what to do, I ask you to fill me with the knowledge of your will in all wisdom and Spiritual understanding, that I may live a life worthy of you, bearing fruit in every good work, and increasing in the knowledge of you in Jesus name Amen!!

6.

FEAR NOT!!

So do not fear, for I am with you; do not be dismayed, for I am your God. I will strength you and help you; I will uphold you with my righteous right hand. Isa 41:10(NIV)

GOD TOLD THE PROPHET ISAIAH THOSE WORDS AS he was about to embark on a journey warning Judah and Jerusalem of their impending destruction as punishment for their sins...But he also spoke of a Messiah that will die for those sins, and the restoration of Israel. Isaiah spoke also, of our Salvation that will take place and an Eternal Kingdom to come, that we all would have access to by inviting his son Jesus as Lord and savior. Like God foreknew Isaiah he also foreknew you and I. We all have a mission and purpose in life whether we find it or not it's there. Every day I continue to learn more and more about my own gifts. But whatever that is we're all assigned a journey. I believe the reason we ought to seek God in our assigned and purpose journey is to avoid any pitfalls along the way.

Prayer~~ Lord God just like you've called Isaiah so you've also called me. Thank you for making me strong and fearless in pursuit of whatever you've called me to do. I will continue to be strong in the Lord and in the power of your might in Jesus Mighty name Amen!!

7.

BE HUMBLE!

"Humble yourselves in the sight of the Lord, and he shall lift you up... **James 4:10 NIV**

ALLOW ME TO REFERENCE THESE POINTS OF SCRIP-tures that speaks for itself an should be void of any commentary. Here in Luke 18:10-14 Jesus speaks a parable, two men went up to pray, one a Pharisee and the other a tax collector. The Pharisee stood by himself and prayed God I thank you that I am not like other people, robbers, evildoers, adulterers, or even like this tax collector. I fast twice a week and give a tenth of all I get. Vs 13 But the tax collector stood at a distance. He would not even look up to heaven, but beat his breast and said, God, have mercy on me, a sinner...Vs 14 I tell you that this man, rather than the other, went home justified before God. For all those who exalt themselves will be humble and those who humble themselves will be exalted.

A proud man is full of himself, but a humble man is full of God. Humility looks good on everyone, wear it proudly.

Prayer~~ Lord God I praise your Holy name as I humble myself before you, submissive and ready to be led. My eyes and ears are open an attentive, for only you will guide me through the right path for my life. I understand that true humility is knowing that I am nothing without you, but I am everything with and in you...In Jesus name Amen!!

8.

GOD'S GRACE

But by the grace of God I am what I am,
and his grace to me was not without effect...
no I worked harder than all of them – yet
not I, but the Grace of God was with me.
1 Cor15:10 NIV

HERE PAUL ATTRIBUTES TO THE GRACE OF GOD. HIS
point is so well taken. Paul is saying yes, I've paid a price
my dues accounted for, but I couldn't do it without the
unmerited favor of God (Grace) on my life. Paul has suffered immensely for the good of the gospel. Even carrying
a thorn in his side which God proclaimed his grace is all he
needed 2Cor12:9.

God's Grace is also sufficient for you and I. Don't be
quick to give up that's as simple as I will try to say it. Every
success comes with a price. A preacher once said you'll
never know what you can do or how far you can go in life
if you never put a demand on your potential. With God's
grace and your potential, it's like his super on your natural
but you got to do something. God is never in nothing but
he's always in something.

Prayer~~ Lord I thank you that your grace is limitless in my life, it surrounds me wherever I go and in everything I do. I believe your grace is causing full manifestation in my life in every area, Supernatural Increase, promotion, restoration, preferential treatment are all beautiful attributes of your nature. Thank you, Lord, for being that source of supply always in my life in Jesus name Amen!!

9.

GOD'S FAVOR!

But the Lord was with Joseph, and showed him mercy, and gave him favor in the sight of the keeper of the prison...**Gen 39:21 NIV**

LIKE JOSEPH, LIKE DAVID, LIKE HANNAH, LIKE Daniel like so many examples of God's amazing favor throughout the Bible. Always remember there is in fact a set time of God's favor on your life also. Because you're the righteousness of God you're entitled to his covenant kindness and favor. Please remember his favor surrounds us wherever we go and in everything we do. What God has already purposed for your life no one can annul it. Like I say for myself many times I am saying to you, stay in faith, one thrust of God's favor can catapult you to places you would never think possible, so cast not away your confidence which has great recompence of reward. Heb 10:35

Prayer~~ Father I thank you that I have found favor with you in all that you've made me to be, I thank you that the light of your favor will come bursting in my life, causing full manifestation in every area. Supernatural Increase, preferential treatment, promotion, restoration. I thank you for continuing to be that source of supply. I will always walk in the favor of God and in the comfort of the Holy Ghost Amen and Amen!!

10.

HE'S ABLE

Again, I say unto you, that if two of you shall agree on earth as touching anything that they shall ask, it shall be done for them of my father which is in heaven... **Matt 18:19 NIV**

YES, OUR GOD IS ABLE THEREFORE THINK BIG, believe, agree, whatever you desire for, believe for have faith for because there he is in the midst putting those truths to reality. I keep reminding myself the love that God has for me I believe you should do the same he is your source of everything ...a faithful father who is the center of your life or wants to be.

Prayer~~ Father, in the name of Jesus this is indeed the confidence that we have in you that if we ask anything according to your will you will do it. I am confident and bold to show up at your throne of Grace with open arms to receive all that you have prepared for me in Jesus name...Amen!!

11.

GOD IS YOUR "I AM"

God said to Moses," This is what you are to say to the Israelites: 'I AM has sent me to you.'" **Exo 3:14 NIV**

WHEN MOSES ENCOUNTERED GOD ON MOUNT Horeb, the bush was on fire, but it was not consumed by the flames. At this location Moses was appointed by God to lead Israel out of Egypt and into the land of Canaan. When Moses asks God, what should I say to these people when they ask me who sent you, God [Elohim] replies "I AM who I AM sent you... The significance to that response is really predicated on the truth that God will be any and everything you want him to be. Healing, deliverance, peace, prosperity, success... whatever it is that you need to address, the truth of his promises shall not return void. Take a moment and understand that he is more than your God but a friend. God equates friendship this deep; "Greater love hath no man than this, that a man lay down his life for his friends... John 15:13. I believe if you let him, the love of God will enfold you, the power of God will protect you and his presence will watch over you so where ever you are He is!!

Prayer~~~Lord I thank you that "I AM" is all that is sufficient for me, before I was formed in my mother's womb you knew me and already had prepared a way for me. Thank you for being my way maker, my covenant keeper, my light in the darkness, equipping me with all that I need to fulfill my destiny in Jesus Name Amen!!

12.

GOD'S PLANS AND PURPOSE FOR YOU

For I know the plans I have for you," declares the Lord, "Plans to prosper you and not to harm you, plans to give you hope and a future...**Jer 29:11 NIV**

LET ME START BY SAYING YOU'RE NOT A MISTAKE, a freak of nature, an accident, none of what seems to infiltrate some people's minds of egregious self-identifiers. You are made in the image of God almighty. Even if your parents didn't plan you God had a plan and a purpose for you and it's for your good an expected end. Even when you're in pain there is purpose, reasons for your struggles, but God will reward your faithfulness, so I urge you to stay in faith with an expectation of God's promises to you.

Prayer~~~ Lord I thank you that I live my life in great expectations of what lies ahead. I Know the plans you have for me is good, not to harm me but to give me hope a future and an expected end. I know you've created me for a purpose. I was not born to be a loser but born to win and reign in life in Jesus name Amen!!

13.

SURRENDERING

Do not conform to the pattern of this world but be transformed by the renewing of your mind. Then you will be able to test and approve what God's will is his good, pleasing and perfect will...**Rom 12:2 NIV**

THIS SCRIPT COULD BE APPLIED IN SO MANY FOR- mats. I believe if you surrender your total being to God, he will completely transform you. I am referencing this based on my own experiences with God. As an adolescent living in New York, I lived for the most part a lascivious lifestyle, the life of the party if you may, then the Lord spoke to my Spirit, son it's time to leave, but for me that was the beginning of a warring moment with my flesh and it wouldn't have any of it. One thing that I've experienced is that God when he loves you, as he does you, he would not give up on you or take no for an answer. Yes, for a while I ignored everything associated with relocating but it had to take a threat on my very existence for me to get the message. The desire to comply was in full effect. I got to the point where I was telling everyone about homes in Atlanta that was practically looking for me.

It became so funny even I couldn't understand the impulses I now had to move to a city God's placed in my heart that I had no affiliation with. But It's there that I got saved an began a campaign of serving the lord, praying for folks in need of prayer, interceding on behalf of others, I've also learned that God will change you and you wouldn't even know you're changing until you've changed. What an experience! Partner with him, Jesus Christ in you and we in him...Gal3:20

Prayer ~~~ Lord as I face every new day, I understand that new mercies are available to me every morning. I thank you for the work you have done in my life and are continuing to do...I surrender every part of my being to you; I thank you for transforming me as I continue to keep my heart and mind stayed on you in Jesus name Amen!!

14.

FORGIVENESS

For if you do not forgive others when they sin against you, your heavenly father would not forgive you. Vs15 But if you forgive others their sins, your father will also forgive your sins... **Matt6:14-15**

SOME OR EVEN MOST OF US HAVE STRUGGLED with unforgiveness at some point in our lives feeling betrayed and victimized and for some folks it still is an ongoing phenomenon. Jesus made it clear in that script, in an effort to free us from unforgiveness you must forgive others or your heavenly father just won't forgive you. Even for me it took time for me to understand how impactful not forgiving others hinders your progress with God. He cannot work with you or move you forward so the truth is it's really for you, yes you've been hurt maybe humiliated but God sees the injustices, the hurts, even the humiliation it may have caused you, but he promises to restore that, fix that, even make amends. So, look at it as forgiveness being for you so that God can in fact make you to be all that he's created you to be, don't be held in bondage. Your success, your healing, your prosperity could all hang in the balance. Remember God knows how to vindicate you.

Prayer~~ Lord Forgive me for the times I never understood the true value of forgiveness, now that I am enlightened with understanding I proclaim every burden be removed and yokes destroyed paving the way for a successful and promising future in Jesus Name Amen!!

15.

GOD IS FAITHFUL

God is faithful, who has called you into fel-
lowship with his son, Jesus Christ our Lord...
1 Cor 1:9 NIV

IN 1COR PAUL TEACHES ABOUT MANY THINGS'
marriage, Christian liberties, Spiritual gifts, the resurrection
of the dead, charity, love, things of that nature, but here
I believe in this letter to Timothy from Paul to the Corinth
church was a letter of encouragement reminding him that
God has called you to be a Faithful servant. Here Paul prays
for them about many things also reminding them of God's
faithfulness and that there be no division amongst them.

Know therefore that the Lord your God is God; he is a
faithful God, keeping his covenant of love to a thousand
generation of those who love him and keep his commandments Deu7:9(NIV)

There are countless scriptures about the faithfulness
of our God. He's given each of us the measure of faith
and even if your faith is as a mustard seed, he reminds us
that it's better than having no faith at all...and even when
you've felt like you've missed a mark we serve a God who's
faithful and just to forgive us of our sins and to cleanse
us from all unrighteousness 1 John1:9. We can also have

hope, because if there is faith we can also hope. Faith is assurance, like a law it will work if you work it. Remember it's never what a situation looks like, it's how you see and approach it through the eyes of faith.

Prayer~~~ Dear heavenly Father thank you for the dreams and desires you've placed in my heart. I choose to trust in you and wait for your plan to bring them to pass. I know you are faithful and I thank you for guiding, instructing and directing my every step in Jesus name Amen!!

16.

GOD IS YOUR HEALER

Heal me Lord, and I will be healed, save me and I will be saved, for you are the one I praise...**Jer 17:14 NIV** also see **Isaiah 53:4-5, Ps 107:20, 1 Pet 2:24, 3 John 2**

ONE OF THE NAMES OF GOD IS JEHOVAH-RAPHA, your healer and the one who makes bitter experiences sweet. The scripture also says he sent his word and healed you forgiving all your iniquities, healing all your diseases and delivering your life from destruction. Ps 107:20. I urge you to meditate on the word of God concerning your healing. The title of this book is to use the word of God as medicine. I believe sickness and disease has no power over the Word and that's why I advise the Word as medicine especially when it comes to your well-being. What good is life if you don't have your health? I have stood on these scriptures that I've noted because It's made a difference in my life. I urge you to meditate day and night feeding your Spirit with the word and speaking life to that sickness, to that disease just like Jesus spoke to that fig tree and it will answer.

Prayer~~~ Lord God you are Jehovah the one who heals me making bitter experiences sweet, thank you for sending your word, I decree and declare that every muscle, every cell, every gland, every bone, every tissue every organ, every system, is functioning in the perfection in which you Lord has created it to function and I decree and declare this to be so in Jesus name I pray Amen!!

17.

GOD YOUR PORTION "FOREVER"

My flesh and my heart may fail, but God is
the strength of my heart and my portion forever. **Ps 73:26 NIV**

THIS PSALM IS ONE OF THE FEW PSALMS THAT WASN'T
written by David. Asaph in the book of Chronicles was one
of three Levites that was commissioned by David to be in
charge of singing in the house of the Lord.

This Psalm speaks to me when I feel like I'm being short
changed. I see God as making up the difference, being
that conduit when I feel that void knowing I can count on
him an no one else to fill that gap.

Many times, my heart failed just trying to do the right
thing, and like many bible characters sometimes even
when you're trying to do the right thing trouble can still
show up. Be it Job, Joseph you may be surprised If I say this
but sometimes, I believe God does allow human suffering
for his own purposes but you'll see the reasons and the vin-
dications afterwards. I recalled some troubles in my own
life and what I can say is that trouble is not necessarily a
sign of sin in a person's life, through some of my trials I did
realize I was drawing closer to God and I believe he may
also be trying to get your attention also, drawing you closer.

Prayer~~~Lord thank you for being all that I'll ever need, filling that gap whenever I feel short changed. I do believe your Blessing over my life is not about the car, the house, money but really an empowerment to prosper in every area of my life. So, if you are my portion, then I lack no good or beneficial thing in Jesus name Amen!!

18.

I AM ONLY CLAY

"Like clay in the hand of the potter, so are you in my hand, O Israel. **Jer18:6 NIV**

CALLED INTO THE MINISTRY AS A YOUTH, JEREMIAH is mocked, sometimes beaten for his prophecies, imprisoned. Then God's demonstration to him at the potter's house of who and what we really are, "Clay" that can be molded into shape. I promise you if you were singled out like Jerimiah in a demonstration like that it might certainly have a resounding effect on your own outlook on life. And I say that presumptuously because you can't take for granted the access of that power that our Creator has over our lives. He's seen you not only in your low estate but our life and times is in his hands.

It's amazing, after years of sinful behavior Jeremiah was sent to prophesy to Israel having them to repent of their sins. Though they weren't trying to hear him, God still gave them forty years before their impending destruction to repent. But with a stiff-necked generation as Moses sometimes call the children of Israel, they still rebelled.

"God is not willing that any man should perish, and he is not slow in keeping his promise, as some understand slowness. Instead he is patient with you, not wanting anyone to perish, but everyone to come to repentance." 2 Pet 3:9

Prayer~~~ Lord I know that my life is in the palm of your hands, it's in you that I live, breathe and have my being. Like the potter, mold me into all that you would have me to be and fill me with a fresh flow of your Holy Spirit power daily in Jesus name Amen!!

19.

GOD IS YOUR SHEPHERD

The Lord is my shepherd, I lack nothing. He makes me to lie down in green pastures, he leads me beside quiet waters, he refreshes my soul. He guides me along the right paths for his name's sake. **Ps 23:1-3 NIV**

HAVE YOU EVER FELT LIKE YOUR LIFE HAS NO DIREC-tion? And there you are silently crying out for that guidance, that direction that you somehow just know you desperately need. Well God is your Jehovah Rohi (Shepherd) that leads you in the paths of righteousness. Like David says he prepares a table before us in the presence of our enemies. Psalm 23:5. Despite wherever David was in life he knew God was with him, so wherever you are heading just know that God is going before you also, he is carefully planning your steps he's been there even before you've thought of it. Nothing limits what he does but he does it for your good. Lean on him like David he's already prepared a place for you, when David wrote the 23 Ps that same intimacy God sees you, and he will direct you in the way in which you should go.

Prayer~~~ Lord I thank you for being my shepherd, my source of strength, my guide, my counsel, my instructor, my direction. I believe I am always divinely guided by you. I believe that I will always take the right turn on the road of life. I believe that you will always make a way where there seem to be no way it's in Jesus Name that I pray Amen Amen!!!

20.

ANGUISHED/STRESSED?

Surely it was for my benefit that I suffered such anguish. In your love you kept me from the pit of destruction; you have put all my sins behind your back. **Isaiah 38:17 NIV**

WHEN WORD CAME TO HEZEKIAH FROM THE prophet Isaiah saying put you house in order you about to die...I can't imagine a more stressful situation and the anguish that ensues. The Bible says Hezekiah wept bitterly, reminding the Lord of all the good he's done in his sight. Today it's so sad that we look around a nation that's crying out for justice social, racial, and economic and though these injustices have plagued this nation from the onset of its founding being a good citizen and having done good in the sight of the Lord, you may say "this doing good stuff benefits me none allow me to take it from here. These injustices like an anchor remains. But there is a higher power that you can weep to. We look to a God that will not only sustain your life, but right injustices. Let us continue to seek the goodness and pleasures of God, continue to hunger and thirst after righteousness. I'll say this, there may be a purpose for your pain, a reason for your struggle but a reward for your faithfulness. God still sits on the throne and he will bring you out of your situation also. Isaiah says he will indeed give you double for your trouble. Isaiah 61:7

Prayer~~~ Lord Jesus I thank you for delivering my soul from anguish, stress, bitterness , bring to mind the people I need to forgive and help not just melt away all bitterness or resentment that I may harbor, but allow my mind, my soul and my Spirit to breathe. I know my life may depend on this so keep me grounded in your promises in Jesus name Amen!!

21.

SWORD OF THE SPIRIT (THE WORD OF GOD)

> Take the helmet of salvation and the sword of the Spirit, which is the Word of God...
> **Eph 6:17 NIV**

I HAVE COME TO LEARN THE POWER IN THE WORD of God. It has become so vital for my own survival. Speaking the Word daily has become that righteous tool that I use to sustain all the indifferences I feel surrounded by. Everybody's got an opinion an opinion here, an opinion there half the time it's not even substantiated by the Word of God but somehow find ears. I tell you if you allow certain non-truths to permeate your being or even other people's truths, that's contrary to righteousness you might as well wait for someone every day to puppet you around. I've even had times when I feel the energy of being marginalized for some of the comments I've made; don't get me wrong I'm not suggesting abuse of authority in any way, authority has its place and must be respected because if you refuse to submit to authority there is not only consequences to that but to the contrary you yourself could not possibly be in authority, so that goes both ways. My point is to always be an advocate for God's Word wherever it may take you because his Word is life. God's Word has allowed me a Spirit of discernment as I intimately look to him daily for inspiration.

Prayer~~~ Father I do understand that our struggle is not against flesh and blood, but against the rulers, against the authorities, against the powers of this dark world and against the spiritual forces of evil in the heavenly realm... That is why I rely on your Word daily to discern your truths from what may be facts knowing that facts are subject to change but the truth of your words remains eternal. So, I thank you Lord that with your words I am able to cast down every stronghold of wrong thinking, of wrong words, Imaginations, pride, deceit, self-pity, anger but abide in your Word daily in Jesus name Amen!!

22.

DELIVERANCE

He shall call upon me, and I will answer him;
I will be with him in trouble, I will deliver him
and honor him. **Ps 91:15 NIV**

MAKE NO MISTAKE GOD IS A DELIVERER, AND HE'S
given us his word as a resource to live by. When we're
facing difficult times like we are right now I could not
imagine calling on anyone else to lean on but the Lord. As
children and believers of God we must rely on his resources.
I've seen the impossible made possible by encouraging
myself in the Lord, he says again "and call on me in the
day of trouble; and I will deliver you, and you will honor
me." Ps 50:19

You have not because you ask not, do not assume the
position that well God knows I'm in trouble he'll do what
he has to do, no we have the privilege of prayer holding
firmly to our faith, prayer changes things. Please do not try
to will power your way into everything you will come to
realize that even the small things God wants to be a part
of to give you an expected end. It's his nature to be good
to us so develop that personal relationship with him.

Prayer~~~ Lord God thank you for delivering me, always being my help in times of trouble. As I pray seeking your face daily, I believe that no weapon formed against me shall ever prosper. I will continue to seek your face always because it's in you that I continue to remind myself that I live, breathe and have my being in Jesus name Amen!!

23.

YOU ARE AN OVERCOMER

For everyone born of God overcomes the world, this is the victory that has overcome the world, even our Faith **1 John 5:4 NIV**

LET IT BECOME A HABIT TO REMIND YOURSELF THAT you are fearfully and wonderfully made, Ps 139:14 loved and protected by God. We were created to dominate in life. God said in Genesis to have dominion over the earth... Be mindful not abuse it! We all have some form of obstacle to hurdle, some situation, some circumstance, but this is a job for you, and for me because there is no Government program that I know of is gonna remove your mountain or there is no such thing as "remove my mountain.com" that's going to bail you out. We must learn how to live and walk by faith. When the dust settles is when we overcome.

Prayer~~~ Lord God, because of my faith I can move mountains. I have no limits in life. I have a positive and winning mindset. I am fearless, I am victorious and with God I can overcome anything. Therefore, I will remain joyful in hope, faithful in affliction and faithful in prayer in Jesus name Amen!!

24.

WORSHIP

Ascribe to the Lord the glory due his name;
bring an offering and come before him.
Worshipping him in the splendor of his holi-
ness! **1 Ch 16:29 NIV**

WE WERE CREATED TO BLESS, WORSHIP AND PRAISE
God always. The Bible says his praise shall continue to be in
our mouths. Blessing the Lord and worshipping him must be
learnt. We function best in his praise and worship, acknowledging him for who he is and what he has done. These
days I try to spend most of my time praising and worshipping him asking him for wisdom, and instruction, even more
so now in this time of uncertainty.

Prayer~~~ Lord God we worship you and Bless your Holy
name ...I was created to praise you and that I will do for all
time. I will continue to greatly rejoice in you, my soul shall
always be joyful for you hath clothed me with your garment of salvation and with the robe of your righteousness
in Jesus name Amen!!

25.

GOD IS MERCIFUL

Who is a God like you, who pardons sin and forgives the transgressions of the remnant of his inheritance? You do not stay angry forever but delight to show mercy...**Micah 7:18 NIV**

OVER 40 TIMES IN THE BIBLE WE KNOW THAT GOD'S love endures forever, but so is his mercy. Allow me to repeat myself, God isn't mad at you, I say God isn't mad at you. In fact, his promise to you is still yes, and Amen 2Cor1:20. Adopt that attitude that he's already prepared your papers, your name whatever else have you, it is finished.

Prayer~~~ Lord I thank you for being the merciful father that you are, slow to anger but full of mercy. Even when I missed a mark you are still indeed faithful and just to forgive me of my sins and to cleanse me from all unrighteousness Glory be your name!!

26.

COMFORTER...

He heals the broken hearted and binds up their wounds. **Psalms 147: 3 NIV**

AFTER MY DIVORCE YEARS AGO, SOMETHING I didn't see coming, but then suddenly there I was in a desperate situation fighting a losing battle as if in a ship with no rudder. We couldn't seem to solve our differences and I weren't in favor of relocation. Never felt so much pain for so long. But then I opened up to the Lord, I remembered going to my pastor breaking down, I think I still have his handkerchief somewhere around after all these years, anyway I consulted with my mentor, he says man you gonna have to take that pain to the alter Bruh (Brother). I've never spent so many days in my prayer closet praying for strength to mend my heart and to heal my pain. But then one day something happened, I felt the pain, the burden, the helplessness, the weakness just subsided away something you can't really explain. Around that same time, I heard a teaching from Bishop Jakes something about "If someone is not willing to grow with you, they cannot go with you" it's as if he was talking to me. You know you can't help but to know that God sees your pain, I just felt God's got me and there is places he needs me to go and things to do. I've done so much in the Ministry for twelve plus years and I'm just beginning. Writing this book my prayer is that someone can read this an know that God has not forgotten them, he sees your pain also but he's the great and resolute comforter.

Prayer~~~ Lord I thank you for being that comfort through all my ups and downs, my pains and sufferings. You promise to heal the broken hearted and to bind up their wounds. Your comfort is true and evident in my life and I also thank you just for being that self-sacrificing love, one that can never be replaced in Jesus name Amen!!

27.

PROVIDER

And my God shall supply all my needs according to his riches of his Glory in Christ Jesus...**Phil 4:19 NIV**

I TRY TO LIVE WITH THE MINDSET THAT NOTHING IS lacking in my life. Anyone that really knows me know I'm always smiling they often ask what are you smiling about? But see when you know something joy can come from that; the scripture also fulfils that promise that the Lord is your Shepherd you shall not want; therefore, you should never be without any good or beneficial thing. I've had people say to me you just got to keep it real, keep it 100. The only 100 for me is God continuing to overflow my cup with his abundance every touch, every time.

Prayer~~~~Lord I thank you that I lack no good or beneficial thing. Your name is Jehovah Gireh the one who sees my needs and provides for them. I also live my life in expectation and in anticipation that you're doing the impossible in me through me and around me as I follow Jesus. Amen!!!

28.

GOD IS LOVE

For God so loved the world that he gave his one and only Son, that whoever believeth in him shall not perish but have eternal life.
John 3:16 NIV

I'VE ALWAYS BELIEVED THE "VALUE" OF A THING IS determined by the price you would pay for such a thing. We all value things differently. I won't spend a dime on some things I've seen people spent thousands on. It may even be a stretch to offer it to me for free. But let me get to my point what I'm trying to say is that "Value is determined by sacrifice", here God sacrificed his only son for the good of my existence so that you and I could live a life to the full and overflow, well for me that's the ultimate sacrifice that demonstrates God's unwavering love for you and I, take a moment to acknowledge that.

Prayer~~~ Father I may not have a screenshot of your plans for me but I do know you love me so whatever you do will be good and I will be Blessed. You also said in 1 John 4:16 whosoever lives in Love lives in God, and God in him, thank you for your unconditional love toward me always Amen and Amen!!

29.

UNSPEAKABLE JOY

Nehemiah said, "Go and enjoy choice food and sweet drinks, and send some to those who have nothing prepared. This is holy to our Lord. Do not grieve, for the joy of the Lord is your strength." **Neh 8:10 NIV**

HERE AS THE PRIEST EZRA READS THE LAW OF THE day Praising the Lord, and his greatness, Israel worshipped the Lord bowing, reverencing this Holy day as some began to weep Nehemiah, the priest Ezra and other leaders reminds the people this is not that day to mourn, weep or grieve this is a Holy Day have fun go eat what you want glorify God **"The Joy of the Lord is your Strength".** The leaders understood the magnitude of the Word of the Lord being reverenced and Glorified that day. No different today true unspeakable joy comes from what you know, and who's you are. Not to be mistaken for happiness which is predicated upon circumstances which can be short lived. Unspeakable joy is one of the Holy Spirit fruits, so in the presence of the Lord and in his Word, you can rest assure the presence of a never-ending joy we can all bear witness to.

Prayer~~~ Holy Spirit I need that joy that only you can give, forgive me for the times that I let circumstances steal that joy and got the best of me. I believe that heaviness is going and joy is on the way. My life is going to be filled with laughter and happiness. The scripture says that I will have joy unspeakable and full of Glory...In Jesus name Amen!!

30.

REJOICING IN THE LORD

Rejoice in the Lord always and again I say rejoice **Phil 4:4 NIV**

WHEN WE UNDERSTAND THAT WORSHIPPING, Praising, Rejoicing and thanking God becomes a daily systemic regimen in our lives, your life will change. As for me I will continue to greatly rejoice in the Lord and again his praise shall always be in my mouth.

Prayer~~ Father my soul rejoices in you always. My soul shall be joyful in my God. For he hath clothed me with the garment of Salvation, the Robe of righteousness, the Sword of the Spirit, the Belt of truth in the light of all eternity my troubles are insignificant and temporary because I rejoice in your name always. Amen!!

31.

GOD'S WILL

We are filled with the knowledge of his will through all the wisdom and understanding that the Spirit gives, so that you may live a life worthy of the Lord and please him in every way: .... **Col1:9-10 NIV**

ONE OF THE THINGS I'VE BEEN DOING RECENTLY and I think I may have mentioned it before is asking God for wisdom, instruction and counsel, for everyday accolades, not just at the job, how you deal with family, but how you intercede with others in general. We're living in such a time that even simple words can take on offense, but see God knows even the smallest details about you and things you may not see coming. I ask him for a head's up, I believe being in the will of God you'll be happy and comfortable doing what you do to the best of your ability.

Prayer~~~ Lord God I understand that I don't know everything, what I do know is that I want to be in your will. Allow me the desires to step out in faith that I may do all that pleases you, for all that is in me is far greater and more powerful than the outside in Jesus name mighty name I pray Amen!!!

32.

HOPE

We have this hope as an anchor for the soul, firm and secure...**Heb 6:19 NIV**

OVER THE YEARS I'VE LISTENED TO SOME EXCELLENT teachers of the gospel spent time at their Ministries and I think it was Joyce Meyers or Pastor Dollar that said quote "Hope is an expectation that something good is about to happen" it's the foundation that faith stands on". So, if you have that negative attitude and don't believe on anything good well see nothing good won't happen for you, and you really can't have faith. So, true because like the scripture says faith is the substance of things hoped for right! Heb11:1

Prayer~~~ Father in the middle of a storm I am setting my hope on you. You fight my battles and are greater than all my enemies. My hope is firm and an anchor to my soul. Nothing I face today is more powerful than you. You are that solid ground beneath my feet. Thank you for surrounding those who surround me and contending with those who contend with me. Give me peace in the presence of my enemies, knowing that you see me and defend me in your love in Jesus Name Amen!!

33.

THANKFULNESS

Pray continually, give thanks in all circumstances; for this is God's will for you in Christ Jesus. **1 Thes 5:17-18 NIV**

I CAN'T STRESS ENOUGH THE IMPORTANCE TO GIVE thanks at all times. Maybe it's just me but I believe God would respectfully give to you more if you have an attitude of gratitude at all times. Here Jesus heals ten men with Leprosy;

> Luke 17:11-19 Now on his way to Jerusalem, Jesus traveled along the border between Samaria and Galilee. 12 As he was going into the village, ten men who had leprosy met him. They stood at a distance 13 and called out in a loud voice," Jesus, Master, have pity on us!". 14 When he saw them, he said, "Go, show yourselves to the priests." And as they went, they were cleansed. 15 One of them, when he saw he was healed, came back, praising God in a loud voice. 16 He threw himself at Jesus feet and thanked him-and he was a Samaritan. 17 Jesus asked, "Were

not all ten cleansed? Where are the other nine? 18 Has no one returned to give praise to God except this foreigner?" 19 Then he said to him, "Rise and go; your faith has made you whole." There is couple of things to note here, here Jesus made this man whole (nothing missing nothing broken) just for returning to praise and worship God, but notice Jesus attributes praising thanking God as faith demonstrated...Glory to God. I've always allowed praising and thanking God as part of my prayer life because I know tomorrow is not promised. I thank him for life, breath, health, strength wisdom all the things that's essential to life and Godliness. And because of that I feel a peace that surpasses all understanding.

Prayer~~~ Lord I will always have an attitude of gratitude for even the smallest of things. I'm Blessed with having the opportunity to praise and worship you day in and day out. Praising and thanking God is who I am and what I do. In Jesus name Amen!!

34.

WE BELONG TO GOD

For in him we live and move and have our being...we are his offspring. **Acts 17:28 NIV**

I THINK MOST PEOPLE WOULD AGREE WITH THE statement that we are all God's children. But the truth is if you're an unrepentant sinner and never made Jesus Lord of your life the word says you're in fact an enemy, see Rom 5:10...For if, while we were God's enemies, we were reconciled to him through the death of his Son, how much more, having been reconciled, shall we be saved through his life!

That is why being born again, is more than to just coexist with his son Jesus. Making Jesus Lord of your life is the pathway to our salvation and a son an heir to the throne. God wants to be there for us, he loves us, he sees our trials, our dilemmas, our situations he listens to our prayers. He wants to be your loving dad; uplifting you in every situation.

Prayer~~~ Lord thank you for always being there for me. I belong to you and as a loving father you are always there to see me through every situation. As I've accepted you as Lord of my life, I know that you will bring me into a flourishing finish, it's in you that I live breathe and have my being in Jesus name Amen!!

35.

A REFLECTION ON PURPOSE

And I thank Christ Jesus our Lord, who hath enabled me, for that he counted me faithful, putting me into the Ministry...**1 Tim 1:12(NIV)**

YOU KNOW I COULD CHOOSE DOZENS OF GOD'S servants who had a God given purpose be it Abraham, Isaac, Jacob, Moses, David, Joseph, Elisha so much to count as I feel short changed of its immensity.

I just happen to choose this script. Timothy who worked alongside now aging Paul was now pastoring a church in Ephesus when he made that statement. Here he's thanking God "Who hath enabled him counting him faithful for the works of the ministry 1 Tim 1:13 . I was reflecting on my own self as I chose that script. God gave us all unique talents for a reason...that being to serve him, so whether you're a surgeon, a Janitor, a hairdresser no one'll do it the way you do. Take the time to consider your own God given talents he has bestowed to you, thanking him for also counting you faithful to pick up that mantle doing your Job as unto the Lord. Remember we were created on purpose for God's purpose.

Prayer~~~ Dear God, I want to live my life serving you and Ministering to others. Give me the wisdom to know which unique gifts you have given me and an understanding of how I can use them to minister. Give me the confidence and strength I need to serve. Whenever I am ministering, help me to do it unto you and not for my own Glory knowing that by faith you will continue to fulfill your unique purpose for my life always in Jesus name Amen!!

36.

WHATEVER YOU ASK

Therefore, I tell you, whatever you ask for in prayer, believe that you have received it, and it will be yours. **Mark 11:24 NIV**

ALSO SEE 1 JOHN5:14 THAT THIS THE CONFIDENCE we have in approaching God: that if we ask anything according to his will, he hears us. And if we know that he hears us- whatever we ask- we know that we have what we asked of him. Key words ask and believe(confidence) well how come!!? So, Jesus told his disciples "Therefore I say unto you, what things so ever ye desire, when you pray, believe that ye receive them and ye shall have them...so now pardon my repetition! See prayer is the key, but it's your faith that unlocks the door. We must pray believing that God is always working in our situation in and out of season for a good an expected outcome...Our Job is to pray and believe that's it. No God doesn't need your help thank you, I think he's got it.

Prayer~~~ Lord you are able to do miracles and work wonders. Remind me of your limitless power. I serve a God who is able to do exceedingly, abundantly moreover than I could ever ask or imagine. My greatest victories are still in front of me! Father may you remove every hindrance and paralyze every power that is against my progress this year. Let my progress be accelerated, and my rewards be in a double portion in your Mighty name Jesus Amen!!

37.

MY HELP COMES FROM ABOVE

But as for me, I am poor and needy, come quickly to me Oh God you are my help and my deliverer; Lord do not delay... **Ps 70:5 NIV**

WE OFTEN HEAR IN CHURCH AND ABOUT, ABOUT the various trials, and tests God's servants faced in light of the Gospel. Though we can never minimize the travails and triumphs of David's life we can sometimes make parallels to our own lives. Psalms 70:5 another psalm attributed to David shockingly reveals a man for the most part of his life in great trouble, turmoil and desperation.

This psalm to me runs a gamut of human emotions which is why I believe so many people turn to them in times of Joy, sadness, sickness and pain. But like David your help also comes from above Ps121:1-2.

Prayer~~~ Lord Jesus you are my help I depend on you. I have no power of my own. In my trials I rely on you. In my temptations I trust in you. My success is in your hands. Save me from all evil and guide my going out and my coming in now and forever more ...Amen!!

38.

I AM THE RIGHTEOUSNESS OF GOD

He made Christ who knew no sin to [judicially] be sin on our behalf, so that in him we would become the righteousness of God in Christ Jesus. **2 Cor5:21 AMP**

ANOTHER TOUCH OF GOD'S UNCONDITIONAL love for us! Here again God's giving up his son for you and I, though we're not deserving, his love for us is immeasurable and he's doing that so that by His death we would be made acceptable to him and placed in a right relationship and standing with God by his gracious, loving, kindness. Our God, my Jesus.

Prayer~~~ Lord God you are Jehovah Tsidkenu my Righteousness, thank you for becoming sin for me that I might become the Righteousness of God in the Annointed one Jesus Christ Amen!!

39.

YOU "GOD'S WORKMANSHIP"

For we are God's workmanship, created in Christ Jesus to do good works, which God pre-pared in advance for us to do. **Eph2:10 NIV**

GOD'S INTENT IS ALWAYS TO ENSHRINE US TO BE more like his son Jesus. In Heb 12 the Bible also says that God is working with us to bring us into a better and more Godly behavior. He not just wants to change our image, but to expand us from a level of Glory to Glory even as the Spirit does. We are in fact destined by God to be molded into the image of Christ. My own story when the Spirit of the Lord moved on my desires in 2003 just a few years later I realized the transformation that took place. One thing that I've learnt and I'll say it again, God will change you and you won't even know you're changing until you've changed. He's even changed my desires, certain words, certain places were just not me no more it's amazing where the Lord will take you for the good of yourself.

Prayer~~~ Father thank you for loving me enough to work in me. I can boldly declare by faith who I am in Christ. Thank you for creating me as one of a kind. Today I choose to believe that I am your workmanship, ever ready to receive in the mighty name of Jesus Amen!

40.

RENEW YOUR MIND

Do not conformed to the pattern of this world, but be transformed by the renewing of your mind. Then you will be able to test and approve what God's will is—his good, pleasing and perfect will...**Rom12:2 NIV**

ONE OF THE MOST INTRIGUING AND APPEALING features of the gospel has to be the ability and the prospect of renewing your mind...He gives us those abilities to change and renew our mind, I've seen my own desires change, a change in the way I think, the way I react, and he's given me wisdom and instruction in more ways than one, guiding and directing every aspect of my life. I always say to folks don't try to will power your way into everything! inquire of God. He will give you the desires of your heart helping you in all that you seek. The truth is when it comes too much to bear forfeit your will and embrace his.

Prayer~~~ Lord God I thank you for a renewed mind. Help me always to ponder the path of my feet, continue to give me a clear vision of what I should do and where I should go at the same time keeping me focused on doing your will. Keep me free from the pleasures of sin...for to that lies the heart of destruction. Allow me to seek the pleasures of God instead and to continue to hunger and thirst after righteousness in Jesus name Amen!!

41.

AUTHORITY

Jesus said to peter, and I will give you the keys to the Kingdom of heaven and whatever you bind on earth will be bound in heaven, and whatever you loose on earth will be loosed in heaven...**Matt 16:19 NIV**

AS A MINISTRY TRAINING AND DEVELOPMENT STU-dent years ago for my graduating class I had to give a 10 min speech if you may on Authority. I remembered quite vividly how passionate I was about this subject. God has given us the authority to replenish the earth subdue it, and to have dominion over all things that moves on the earth **Gen1:25-28.** But because of Adam and Eve's disobedience, the devil stole that authority away from us...Gen 3: 16.

But Jesus; the key point I want to get across is that Jesus didn't just merely die for our sins, he also reconnected us back to every promise of God by shedding his blood. That key that Jesus went to the depths of hell to recover represents our restored authority. He has taken the keys of death and hell and given us the keys of Blessing and life. We need to now acknowledge that authority and with our mouths cut things off that need to be cut off, and purge things that need to be purged and open the windows of heaven. We have the authority to bind and to loose and it is "WHAT WE SAY IT IS"!!

Prayer~~~ Father I thank you that I could come boldly to the throne of Grace because of what Jesus has done. We also acknowledge that according to Matt 16:19 that whatsoever I bind on earth is bound in heaven and whatsoever I loose on earth is loosed in heaven... I thank you Lord for that God given "Restored Authority" to dominate over all things that pertain to life and Godliness in the magnificent name of Jesus Amen!!

42.

GOD IN YOU

You, dear children, are from God and have overcome them, because the one who is in you is greater than the one who is in the world. **1 John 4:4 NIV**

YOU KNOW IF WE CAN WRITE OUR OWN LIFE'S script for tough times, it would be a very positive, generous an optimistic one, more happiness, more joy, feel good endings, diseases cured peace and prosperity for all, in the nick of time fixes. It would be the perfect script. But in times of trouble God may seem invisible and we get frustrated as to why he isn't speaking or doing something. But I promise you he's there. God is not loud; the Bible says he'll speak to you in a still and silent whisper, but are we listening!? A preacher once said if you focus on the ultimate you won't fall victim to the immediate; translation that mountain of circumstances or situation you're in don't compound that situation by giving it life but stay focus on that still small voice. What is God saying!

Prayer~~~ Father give me an ear to hear and a heart to receive. I believe that I will encounter supernatural mani-festation if I stay focused on your still small voice. I believe that the Spirit of revelation will open up my knowledge of who you are and from that comes the release of power from heaven in Jesus name Amen!!

43.

GOD IS YOUR REFUGE

God is our refuge and strength, an ever-present help in trouble. **Ps 46:1 NIV**

TO BE YOUR REFUGE SIMPLY MEANS, YOU'RE SAFE and sheltered under the loving arms of God, from pursuit, danger or trouble. In a time of social, racial, emotional and economic distress and injustices, it's very important to have God be the center and direction of your life and I mean that literally. I can't even begin to imagine not having God to be my cover, an according to his promise no weapon formed against you shall prosper...Isaiah 54:17. In times of despair I urge you to speak with him, spend time in your prayer closet if you have to, Isaiah reminds us to put the Lord in remembrance of his promises, keep not silent... Isa 62:6.

Prayer~~~ Lord God give me peace in the presence of my enemies; knowing that you see my every move and are there to defend me with your loving protection...Thank you for being there in my going out and my coming in in Jesus Name Amen!!

CONTENTMENT

The apostle Paul said, I know what it is to be in need, and I know what it is to have plenty. I have learned the secret of being content in any and every situation... **Phil 4:12 NIV**

GOD WANTS US ALL TO HAVE A PERSONAL RELA-tionship with him, he is not a secret to be kept. He wants to be your lead, guide and help in all your situations keeping you contented during the process. Knowing him personally there is no need to have a reaching mindset he knows the things you are in need of. Somebody said well Brotha Sean if he knows my needs that well why is it that it seems he's never listening! He's listening alright sometimes you just don't want to receive what he's saying. Never be anxious for anything, God's timing is always perfect he's focused on a good expected ending for you and sometimes it involves him getting you out of your own way. Practice fellowshipping with him. Paul has learned that lesson, we all can learn that lesson. And if you think that because you've missed a mark and somehow think that that's a prerequisite for my Joy and contentment, just know he's a faithful God, faithful and just to forgive us of our sins and to cleanse us from all unrighteousness. 1 John 1:9

Prayer~~~ Lord God in whatsoever state I am help me to be contented, for you are my source of supply. Lord use me as your steward wherever you need me today. I am an instrument of your favor; you've made me a light-bearer not to hide under a bucket but to be put on a light stand. I will continue to walk in love for it will always make room for my contentment in Jesus Name Amen!!

45.

SALVATION

God's plan is that all people be saved and to come to a knowledge of the truth...**1Tim2:4**

I WILL CONTINUE TO SAY THIS AGAIN BUT GOD wants us all to have a personal relationship with him... Remember God only leads us to places of Increase, profit, honor, promotion things of value. By spending time with him you obtain that peace, that security, that triumph no matter the opposition, it's our inheritance as a child of God and he's provided a pathway by making Jesus Lord of your life. God knows we are all sinners and that all have sinned and fall short of the glory of God...Rom 3:23 but he's also a loving and faithful God willing to forgive us of our sins and to cleanse us from all unrighteousness...1 John1:9. And remember Salvation is not just about going to heaven it's also about ruling and reigning in your authority, living kingdom minded right here on earth.

Prayer~~~Lord I thank you for my salvation for being a good and faithful father, forgiving all my sins, cleansing me from all unrighteousness, healing every wound and bruise of my soul. Thank you for watching over my going out and my coming in now and forevermore Amen!!

WE ARE STRENGTHENED

We are strengthened with all power, according to his Glorious might, so that you may have great endurance and patience giving joyful thanks to the father, who has qualified you to share in the inheritance of his holy people in the kingdom of light...
Col 1:11-12

I DON'T' KNOW ABOUT YOU BUT BEING A STUDENT of the Bible I've always contemplated on what as Moses called the children of Israel at times a stiff-necked people. Though they've seen so many of God's miracles from the plagues on Pharoah, parting of the red sea, manna from heaven you name it. Yet apart from Joshua and Caleb no one seem to esteem themselves more than just mere men, they even self-identified themselves as grasshoppers.

It's very important that we emulate the attitudes and strength of a Joshua or a Caleb these days. God reminds us that we are in fact strengthened with all might according to his glorious power within.

God told the Israelites to be strong and of good courage for I am with you. Look I understand that even if you feel you're an expert, fear doesn't necessarily go away with a tough task at hand...but I believe that accepting fear as part of any journey that helps you to conquer it. To go anywhere you must launch out from somewhere. Trust the God strength in you.

Prayer~~~Lord I thank you that I am strong in the Lord and in the power of your might, I am not moved by what I see or anything that's contrary to the word of God, I am only moved by what I believe and I believe the word of God, I step out in faith knowing that no weapon formed against me shall ever prosper. It is You who arms me with strength and keeps my way secure in Jesus name Amen!!

47.

PEACE

Peace I leave with you; my peace I give you... I do not give to you as the world gives. Do not let your heart be troubled and do not be afraid. **John 14:27 NIV**

GOD SAYS HE WILL GIVE US A PEACE THAT SUR-passes all understanding. That means a peace not like the world gives but a peace that we can't imagine or compass. I experienced that peace before where I had every right to be out of my mind but the calm and serenity of letting go and letting God proved supreme. One of the names of God is Shalom that peace will also mount garrison over your heart and mind in Christ Jesus. The Bible says let peace rule like an umpire. Col 3:15

Prayer~~~ Father I thank you me and my family dwells in a peaceful habitation, in safe dwellings; and in quiet resting places and that there is stability in our times. I thank you for being gracious to all families covering them always in the mighty name of Jesus...Amen!!!

48.

BOLDNESS

Let us then approach God's throne of grace with confidence, so that we may receive mercy and find grace to help us in our time of need. **Heb 4:16**

THE WORD IS CLEAR COME BOLDLY TO THE THRONE of grace not haphazardly but boldly expecting to hear from God and receive help in a time of need or trouble. Remember God is a merciful God, his mercy is his grace manifested. We have that Blood bought right to come to his throne of grace. Please understand grace is God's unmerited favor towards us. No: you don't have to work for it! Though undeserved it is freely available, don't allow the devil to take off with that promise reminding you about inequities and misdeeds from 20 years ago. Stay focused on all that God has the ability to restore. While we're out there being distracted, the devil is out there stealing your confidence simultaneously. Stay focused. Be engaged.

Prayer~~ Lord thank you for giving me the Spirit of boldness and enabling me to approach your throne of grace with confidence. My soul thirsts for you. In this dry and parched land, I have seen your sanctuary and gazed upon your power and glory. Your unfailing love is better than life itself. As I'm wrapped in your cover of love remind me that I am always safe in your arms in Jesus name Amen!!

49.

YOU ARE NOT A MISTAKE

Ye was chosen before the creation of the world, but was revealed in these last times for your sake. **1 Peter 1: 20 NIV**

IF YOU'RE SITTING THERE CONTEMPLATING ABOUT the purpose of your existence your answer is really to Glorify God and your purpose will justify your existence. A doctor once conveyed an experiment demonstrating the millions of sperm cells it would actually take for you to make it to finish line (The egg). What am I saying; well like the word says we were predestined before the foundation of the world to be here, even at such a time as this?

I like to say if God gave us a blueprint for our lives with all the details, we won't need to exercise our faith, now would we? I accept the fact that I am one of a kind and that there is no carbon copy of me, you should too. Just know that you were in fact created for a purpose. If I get one person to read this book and believe on it, I would have done a good deed. Allow me to remind you, you can uplift yourself even in your low esteem, don't repeat what the enemy may say, Bless yourself with faith filled words like I'm fearfully and wonderfully made, I am anointed, appointed, equipped, strong, empowered to prosper, I am redeemed, loved, God's masterpiece, healed, whole, destined, delivered, mighty, creative, encouraged remind God that you are in agreement with all that he's called you and made you to be. I've said it before we can have all the plans in the world, but it will be the Lord's purpose that will ultimately prevail.

Prayer~~~Father in the name of Jesus I thank you that because you foreknew who I was before the foundation of the world I understand that I was also created to win and reign in life. I am your friend, a covenant partner and an heir with your son Christ Jesus Amen!!

50.

WE'RE ANOINTED

We're anointed with the Holy Ghost and with power, and we go about doing good healing all who were under the power of the devil. **Acts10:38 NIV**

LIKE EVERYTHING IN LIFE FOR SOMETHING TO WORK effective it has to be developed, the same goes for your Spirit. If you have an underdeveloped, malnourished Spirit you simply can't hear from God for he is a Spirit. So, while we may be anointed with power for that to me made manifest and truly become developed, we must spend time in his "Word" it changes the way you think so that your Spirit could be in tune with the word.

God's words confirm and feeds our Spirit man, as we continue to stay in the word that anointing removes burdens and destroy yokes.

Prayer~~~Father give me the desire to meditate on your word daily, I know that the more time I spend in your word, I will see the bridge to physical manifestation in my life. It will become that bridge to my prosperity in mind, Spirit, and soul in Jesus name I pray Amen!!

I AM REDEEMED

> Christ hath redeemed us from the curse of the law, by becoming a curse for us, for it is written: "Cursed is everyone who is hung on a pole." **Gal 3:13 NIV**

THE CURSE OF SIN STARTED THE DAY OF ADAM AND Eve's disobedience in the garden and because of man's fallen nature, God's plan was already implemented as to how that authority would be restored and that we would be in need of a redeemer. But until then, laws were put in place to really keep the children of Israel in check, with sacrifices made to atone for their sins, commandments, but though those laws were intended to keep them aware and to know the knowledge of their sins, they couldn't stop sinning anyway. So, we definitely needed Jesus to redeem us. God's design an intention was for us to be like little Gods of the earth but that obviously didn't pan out. Different teachers explain this process differently but this is my best and simplest way of addressing that.

So, our eternity depended on the last Adam (Jesus), to restore us back to our rightful place, and that redeemer is Jesus Christ our Lord. Jesus says I am the way the truth and the life, no man cometh unto the father but by me:

John 14:6. If you're not born again, you're still living under the dispensation of the law, translation "A curse".

It's Christ who hath redeemed us from that curse. Therefore, accept Jesus as your Lord and live in his marvelous light. It's always going to be what Jesus has done and if we're born again, we're in him and made right with God by our faith in his son, never by obeying the law.

Prayer~~~Heavenly father, I know that I have been redeemed and made righteous by accepting Jesus as Lord of my life. I accept that except a man be born again he cannot enter into your kingdom. I thank you for changing my desires by practicing your presence every day in my life. I will continue to strive to be like my heavenly father making a positive difference in the world...Amen!

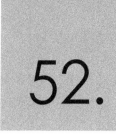

52.

GOD IS YOUR SOURCE OF STRENGTH

For thus saith the Lord God the Holy one of Israel, "In repentance and rest is your salvation, in quietness and trust is your strength, but you would have none of it. **Isaiah 30:15 NIV** see also **Col 1:11-12 NIV**

HERE THE LORD SENDS THE PROPHET ISAIAH TO warn Judah of its impending destruction, instead of trusting in their Lord, this unrelenting and rebellious Israelites called upon Egypt for help. Isaiah used words like destruction, demise, calamity to kind of get their attention but they weren't having it. It's like us sometimes where we'd rather dismiss warner's as overzealous customers not worthy of an ear so we can sin in peace. Sorry I said that sarcastically, but Isaiah spoke with authority and I'm sure he'd made some a few sleepless nights...

In times of trouble we must seek God, when you entertain other solutions, that problem not only magnifies and compounds but you begin going down a slippery slope at your own peril. Look to God that's where our strength lies.

Prayer~~~Lord God I ask and pray that I seek your face always, in times of trouble I know you are my present help. I'm not moved by what I see, or moved by other people's opinions that's contrary to righteousness. I'm only moved by what I believe and I believe the word of God in Jesus name Amen!

53.

SELF-CONTROL (TEMPERANCE)

For this very reason, make every effort to add to your faith goodness: and to goodness, knowledge, and to knowledge self-control; and to self-control; perseverance; and to perseverance, godliness; and to godliness, mutual affection; and to mutual affection, love. **2 Pet 1:5-7 NIV**

I BELIEVE THE CHRISTIAN QUALITIES OF FAITH, VIRTUE, knowledge, self-control, patience, godliness, love coupled with having complete understanding and reliance on God's word can speak volumes in our lives. I am sure we all have battled one or more of these attributes. What I've learned over the years with my impatience is that God would actually put me in an impatient situation and allow me to work my way out of it and for all the times I've failed guess what; I've had to circle that mountain and repeat that class until I passed it is that you? I believe and it might just be me but I believe if you can discipline yourself where self-control is concerned, it lays a case for some of the others. What say you?

Prayer~~~Lord God Instill in me the virtues that I need to be pleasing to you, you said in all things we are more than conquerors Through him that loves us and I am well able to be the best in every aspect of my being through Jesus Christ Amen!!

54.

CONFIDENCE VS OBEDIENCE
(A DISCUSSION)

HERE WE'RE JUST TALKING COULD WE!! COULD YOU have confidence in your obedience to do a thing? I believe so but that doesn't make the two the same, I think they're a dichotomy of one another. Well Jesus had the same approach as he showed confidence in people of the world to turn them from their sinful ways. God's confidence in us is that he has the ability to work in and through us. When you have Christ the world, social media all that stuff no longer becomes the standard but God in all his righteousness stands supreme. But you still have to have a willing, teachable, and have an obedient heart to receive. See I believe God can work in and through all of us yes, if you let him. In revelations 3:20 Jesus say look I stand here at the door knocking but would you be obedient to let him in. God has given us all a free will to choose he's not going to legislate your heart, and take those liberties away. I think there lies the difference, but like I said there may be a difference of opinions but like I said we're just talking. Let's just leave it at that. I know God treasures obedience, he'll take you places you couldn't conceive or imagine, let us just be conscious of that.

Let's pray... Father I Bless every man, woman and child and declare that they can hear the voice of the good Shepherd and the voice of a stranger they will not follow. Help them to stay focus, resolute and confident, fill them with your peace, truth, love and unity having your ever-increasing presence always in Jesus name Amen!!

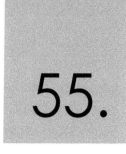

55.

GOD RESTORES

And "I will repay you for the years the locusts have eaten—the great locust, and the young locust, the other locusts and the locust swarm—my great army that I sent among you. **Joel 2:25 NIV**

ALLOW ME THE OPPORTUNITY AGAIN TO VOUCH for my God right here...I promise you, I'm not "gonna" 'and please allow my contraction, say verily, verily, but I will just say let God restore your stuff, how's that. God is a restorer and a vindicator, if you like 100- and 1000-folds increases on your return on your little stuff you've lost well then smile and wait. Look I understand, I've been swindled before, taken advantage of, I've bought a well packaged TV off the streets of NY in the 80's wrapped in plastic and fitted with foam to perfection in a beautifully labelled box that turned out to be a rock. Yes, funny alright only in NY but experience is also a good teacher believe that.

My Pastor once told us a story of giving away some of his best suits not the choice one's mind you, it's funny because he was reminding God that those were the best ones he's got as if God didn't know, anyway again there is so much to say about obedience. Fast forward today Pastor's got so much suits with literally the shoes to match.

What am I saying? I'm saying God wants to take care of you forget your past run ins, God is gracious, generous, loving. Test him and see in the toughest of times, God's nature is always evident. I gave money received double, gave love received even more. God matches your action with a corresponding reaction to infinity, watch this, he even restores loses that you've even forgotten about now that a God right there! When you see restoration just rejoice and be glad, when and even in the midst of your calamities still rejoice even then restoration starts to take effect. That last stuff right there though is for the mature.

Prayer~~~Lord you've seen my good deeds, my story is an open book to you, all that the enemy thought he's stolen will be restored back to me 100 – 1000-fold. Regardless of my situation I will continue to rejoice in the Lord because I know there is power in rejoicing, my heartfelt thanks in Anticipation of an expected return in all that the devil had stolen in Jesus Mighty Name Amen!!

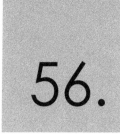

YOU'RE GIFTED

> Every good and perfect gift comes from above, coming down from the father of heavenly lights, who does not change like shifting shadows..." **James 1:17(NIV)**

ALLOW ME TO MAKE A QUICK REFERENCE BACK TO my chapter on "You're not a Mistake" because if God knew and created you from the foundations of the world, he knew you were coming and therefore you came from above, so you're good and perfect in his sight. God has made each of us different in our own uniqueness, there is no carbon copy of you, and I believe you'll appreciate life even more rather than trying hard to be somebody you're not. Understanding your gift, I believe will make room for you...doors will be open. God's gift is working through you and it's good and perfect. The Bishop T.D Jakes once said quote "Every gift has a weakness" I got to thinking how on earth, what do he mean if every gift is perfect how could there be a weakness!? Then he says well you weren't gifted for everything. A reverberated effect went through me like, you know what Mr. Bishop Sir you sure right, because I ain't your brain surgeon, your rocket scientist, pilot see It's also what Paul was trying to say when he basically said stay in your lane, run your race that's set before you." Heb12:1 And the same goes for you, are you running in someone's lane? And wondering why you could never get it right. Now don't get me wrong there is learned behaviors in every endeavor, but to be all that God has created you to be must be found; in a pursuit of what that is, I believe you will find that effortless desire that will certainly make room for you.

Let's Pray~~~ Father I thank you for sharing a light on my special gift. I thank you that it's by your Grace that I was created to be all that you've created me to be. I thank you that my gift will not only make room for me but to help others seeking me to be a Blessing to them and it's in Jesus name that I believe that Amen!!

57.

THE UNCTION TO FUNCTION

But Ye have an unction from the Holy One,
and ye know all things. **1 John 2:20 KJV**

IF YOU'RE IN CHRIST YOU'RE ALREADY ANOINTED
...there is an anointing in your personality that makes you a
distinct person. As the word says you have an unction from
the Holy One and know all things. That word unction comes
from the Greek word "Charisma" or anointing from the Holy
Ghost. Yes with God's anointing over our lives we can function in any area, it's the Holy One that gives us the ability
to know and discern...What I believe God does is apply
his Super on our natural abilities which provides a divine
enablement from God to get the Job done. I believe a
touch of God's power can make you accomplish in no
time what someone else could have taken 20 years to do.
Only with God.

Prayer~~~Lord I thank you for your supernatural ability
operating in, on and through me. That unction gives me
the knowledge to know all things that pertain to life and
Godliness. Because I've kept my focus on you, my char-
acter is protected, giving no room for the enemy to disrupt

my power. That anointing gives me the unction to function in every area of my life in Jesus name Amen!!

58.

TRUSTING IN THE LORD

Trust in the Lord with all thine heart and lean not on your own understanding. In all thy ways acknowledge him, and he shall direct thy paths. **Pro 3:5-6 KJV**

I THINK WE CAN ALL ADMIT THAT IF YOU WERE given the opportunity to design your own life it would probably be the most photogenic picture anyone have ever seen. Why? Well all the things that we agonize about what we could have done better would certainly be omitted making the perfect way for the perfect do over, no sweat, no time or no energy lost. Paul had that mindset though, that we all should adapt; he reminds us that though we may not have it all together we must forget what is behind and straining toward what is ahead. Phi 3:13.

When God fed the children of Israel Manna, they were only to consume for that day all they needed and not to store up. God wants us to trust him with today he wants us to live in the "now". See today is all we have. I believe we must trust our faithful father with our uncertain tomorrow.... looking ahead to all the good and perfect plans he has in store for our lives.

Prayer~~~Lord as I continue to put my trust and faith in you, I will forever be grateful, I do know that my understanding stems from who's I am and who I know, I can still remember all the wondrous deeds you've done in my life because I trusted and believed in you. I will remain committed to you always in Jesus name Amen!!

59.

NO MORE LACK

Then Jesus asked them, "when I sent you without purse, bag or sandals, did you lack anything? "nothing, "they answered.
Luke 22:35 NIV

GOD HAS A SUPERNATURAL WAY TO MAKE SURE you lack nothing, but until you know God takes care of you, in the physical realm I believe you won't suffer lack. I have dozens of nick a time stories. But this one in particular I was out of work years ago for a couple of months, it got to the point my landlord wasn't trying to hear it and he'd started the eviction process. I mean I went on a praying rampage if you may, I even charged my angels that I know is camped round about me to go find work and bring it back, I went all out. Needless to say, weeks later an agency called me she says she has this opportunity at this hospital a hospital that I remembered thinking month's prior what It would be like to work there! Fast forward within a week I was the choice candidate among three contenders. Remember in the meantime still didn't have money still down two months' rent but I got this offer letter from the agency on behalf of the hospital, you know my landlord took that offer letter as collateral and spread my balance for months on end until I became current. Hear me, have you ever heard of such a thing? and watch this It was also around Christmas time; my landlord also brought us $500 worth of Christmas groceries he said he wasn't even sure why he was doing this. Well he may not know but I know. What am I saying? Simply God will take care of you, he will, he will my friends be inspired. If you truly seek and believe God's got you back then let go and let God.

Prayer~~~Father I thank you that I suffer "no lack" because you've got me in the palm of your hands being with me day in and day out. You are my provider and I will boldly declare and shout for joy, be glad and say "let the Lord be exalted who delights in the prosperity of his servant in Jesus name Amen!!

60.

BLESSING MY GOD!!

I will Bless the Lord at all times: his praise shall
continually be in my mouth...**Psalms 34:1 KJV**

I PURPOSELY LEFT THIS FOR LAST BECAUSE IF I CAN
leave you with anything every promise is possible as you
make it a habit of Blessing the Lord, worshipping, Glorifying,
Praising and thanking him. I've allowed that habit to
become second nature in my approach to God. I cannot
even imagine going a day without acknowledging his
presence. For me I always need a fresh flow of his Holy
Ghost power working and living in me. I suggest you do
the same. Thank him for his constant wisdom, instruction,
counsel, guidance, and direction. Again, allow me to
encourage you to see God as he sees you, he loves you
so take that time out of your day to actually let him know
how much you care.

Let's Pray~~~With my soul I will Bless the Lord, and with
every thought and purpose in life. My mind will not wander
out of your presence. I am ever ready to believe the best
of every person. I gird the loins of my mind and keep it set
on what is above. The higher things, not on the things that
are on the earth in Jesus name Amen!!

THE POWER OF GOD'S PROMISES CAN REMOVE burdens and destroy yokes. As I've said in my introduction we live in uncertain and unprecedented times, but I believe it's also a time of reckoning and reform. Take a deep assessment of where you stand in this picture, of who you are and where you're going. Make no mistake you will be judged for those very purpose, and what you've contributed to on this earth. The Bible translates a passage as: "Enter in by the **narrow** gate; for wide is the gate and broad is the **way** that leads to destruction, and many are those who enter in by it". I hope this book can help to alter that direction, rest assure on the promises of God to guide and direct your every step. So be encouraged and do the right thing. At this time, I encourage everyone to stay safe and wear a mask, physical distance, do what you can do to keep yourself and others safe, and God will do what you can't. Remember God honors obedience. Continue to Worship him, Honor him, Praise him, Thank him, Glorify him, Reverencing his Magnificent name at all times.

Be Blessed

CPSIA information can be obtained
at www.ICGtesting.com
Printed in the USA
LVHW072045151020
668921LV00018B/2529